Decisionology

Decisionology

A Guiding Compass for High-School Students

Daniel P. Gates

iUniverse, Inc.
Bloomington

Decisionology
A Guiding Compass for High-School Students

iUniverse books may be ordered through booksellers or by contacting:

iUniverse
1663 Liberty Drive
Bloomington, IN 47403
www.iuniverse.com
1-800-Authors (1-800-288-4677)

Because of the dynamic nature of the Internet, any web addresses or links contained in this book may have changed since publication and may no longer be valid. The views expressed in this work are solely those of the author and do not necessarily reflect the views of the publisher, and the publisher hereby disclaims any responsibility for them.

Any people depicted in stock imagery provided by Thinkstock are models, and such images are being used for illustrative purposes only.
Certain stock imagery © Thinkstock.

ISBN: 978-1-4759-2896-9 (sc)
ISBN: 978-1-4759-2897-6 (hc)
ISBN: 978-1-4759-2898-3 (ebk)

Library of Congress Control Number: 2012909681

Printed in the United States of America

iUniverse rev. date: 07/17/2012

Contents

Foreword

I first came to know Dan Gates in the small southwestern town of Anaconda, Montana, while we were in high school. We played football, ran track, and enjoyed the kind of camaraderie that young, carefree boys in high school often enjoy. We both went to the University of Montana, where we remained friends. Once out of school, we lost touch and saw each other only occasionally. After college, Dan became a successful insurance agent, ultimately owning his own brokerage business, and I went on to law school.

After law school, I prosecuted all types of cases for approximately sixteen years. I was appointed a trial judge in 1988 and have since presided for more than twenty-three years. In my roughly forty years of observing, prosecuting, and sitting on criminal trials, I have seen firsthand the results of the decision-making processes in which people engage. Involvement in the criminal-justice system, youth court, and dependent and neglect matters yields a certain degree of expertise in the consequences of young people's decision making. Unfortunately, observing such consequences does not always result in the ability to communicate the risks of poor decisions with the younger generation or even the parents of the younger generation. That's where Dan's book, *Decisionology*, really brings the music to the show.

Dan Gates became a successful businessman by making the right decisions as a young man and recognizing the poor decisions. Dan grew up in a smelter town, where young people had to make their own fun while their parents tried to scratch out a living. The young people had organized sports and some youth dances, but otherwise they were pretty much on their own; they had to find their own fun as they saw fit and deemed appropriate. The difficult decisions in those days often involved alcohol, but there were also many other decisions promising immediate gratification. These decisions often started a chain of events that would have been so simple to avoid if only the young person had been given some insight or warning about the decision-making process that was about to unfold.

All of us, no matter what our family background, have lost friends and family members because of wrong decisions concerning alcohol. We have all observed some unfortunate soul seemingly lose direction after an unforeseen event that would not have occurred if the person had been prepared for the decision he or she suddenly had to confront.

If an individual makes the right decisions in high school, the pattern seems to be set for more positive decisions in the future, whether in college, vocational school, apprentice training, the military, or other pursuits. Dan Gates humanizes the "decisionology" that our younger generation faces. What Dan has accomplished throughout his life is partially due to his courage in making tough decisions and getting back on track when he found himself occasionally off course.

Parents' job is to give their children a moral compass, which is similar to a GPS. When a young person drifts off course, the moral compass will lead him or her back to the true course.

Decisionology should be mandatory reading for both parents and children. It emphasizes the consequences of decisions, and, more important, it prepares students and parents for the decisions that are certainly coming.

Ed McLean

Ed McLean is a 1973 graduate of the University of Montana Law School. He is a former prosecutor who has prosecuted every type of major felony. Ed has been a trial judge in a court of unlimited jurisdiction (all felonies and civil cases that have no limits on the amount of damages that can be awarded) since 1989 and is presently running unopposed for his fifth six-year term.

Acknowledgments

To my son, Seane Travis Gates, thank you for all the love and support you've shown me throughout your life, regardless of my absence during most of your formative years. Thank you for always being there during both difficult and happy times and for the tenacity and courage you demonstrated in pursuing your college education at the University of Montana. I could not have been more proud the day I witnessed you receiving your diploma and realized that you had matured into a fine young man.

I would also like to acknowledge my brothers Ned and Roy Gates, of whom I have fond childhood memories. In memoriam, I would like to thank my exceptional mother, Helen, who did an amazing job of raising five children on less than one hundred dollars per week. I would also like to thank my father, John C. Gates, who was the best father a son could ask for. He built our three-bedroom home for less than $1,000, thanks mostly to his amazing ingenuity and incredible ability to salvage discarded items and transform them into useable materials. And I would like to thank my sister, Nancy Gates, for being such a special young lady and showing the world how honesty and sincerity, coupled with dogged determination, will always win out. Last but certainly not least, I would like to remember our brother Johnny, one of the kindest and gentlest human beings I have ever had the privilege to know.

Introduction

My fascination with decisions and the decision-making process dates back to my freshman year at the University of Montana. I was working four part-time jobs to help pay for my education and found myself surrounded by four top-flight executives: an attorney, the owner of a car dealership, a sociology professor, and a ranking professor in the zoology department. You guessed it—they were my bosses for the fall quarter, and their decision-making processes all seemed different yet intriguing. The attorney seemed to make decisions rather quickly based upon his grasp of the situation—it almost seemed as if decision making was an automatic response. The sociology professor would often delegate his decisions to his secretary and would occasionally ask me for a progress update. The car dealer chose to consult often with his on-staff accountant, his sales manager, or his office manager regarding all types of decisions. I became fascinated not only with the decisions themselves but with the decision-making methods and strategies. I quickly saw that the power and ability to make good decisions was an essential skill that could translate into success for anyone willing and able to learn.

I owned and personally operated an independent insurance brokerage business for many years, making all kinds of decisions on a daily basis. These decisions ranged from simple to very complex and often had the potential to impact the future welfare of entire families. I personally witnessed the consequences resulting from good and poor decisions in many people's lives.

For example, a twenty-eight-year-old family man with a wife and three children under age ten chose to change his life-insurance protection from $10,000 to $160,000 to more adequately protect his family in the case of his premature death. He was a sawyer in the woods, and even though he was very skilled at his job, he felt that in the late seventies $160,000 would offer the right amount of protection. He recognized the danger in his job and made the decision to do something about it. I am very sad to say that a few short years later, this young man was killed in a tragic logging accident. Money will certainly never replace a loved one, but the additional $150,000 made a huge difference in how this young family was able to go on. The young father made a decision that ultimately had a critical impact on his family's future.

In another situation, a nice married man chose to purchase a new $100,000 life-insurance policy and terminate his existing $10,000 policy. He had recently obtained his private pilot's license, and, in order to qualify for his new $100,000 policy, he had to either pay a higher risk premium or sign an aviation waiver, which specifies that no protection will be provided in the event of death while piloting a private craft. I strongly encouraged him to retain his original policy and simply add the additional protection, but he was adamantly opposed to paying for two policies; he felt the risk was very minimal that he would be killed in a private plane crash. He made the decision to sign the aviation waiver and drop his existing $10,000 policy. I am very sorry to report that he was killed in a private plane crash a few short years later. His decision to drop his initial protection and not pay the higher risk premium ended up dearly costing his wife—she had no life insurance to pay for her husband's funeral.

I saw the life-changing end results of decisions made by people from all walks of life. I witnessed the sadness and sorrow of poor decisions and the joy and appreciation of better decisions. I became acutely aware of the consequences that even small decisions can have.

I have spent the past forty years analyzing, studying, and practicing making decisions, and I have read many books that have helped me understand how to make better decisions and that have illuminated the critical significance of decision-making consequences. I intend this guide to be a simple resource that you can utilize whenever you are presented with challenges or decisions that must be addressed. It is not designed to provide the answers required in a given situation; rather, it will make you aware of the many different types of decisions that are available and the potential consequences they may bring. It is a starting point, a tool that can steer you in the right direction and help you decide when to consult an expert and when to go it alone. Let this guide remind you that the decisions you make can, and do, have an impact and that they will ultimately determine whether you succeed or fail in your future endeavors. Of course, you must own your decisions, which means being willing to be held accountable for the outcomes. It takes only one bad decision to dramatically change the course of your life, as well as the lives of other human beings. Please keep in mind that this guide is not meant to be an all-encompassing discussion of every aspect of the decision-making process; rather, it is meant to serve as a reference to assist you in some of your daily dilemmas.

You must make a habit of *thinking* before acting and making decisions whenever possible. We all make spur-of-the-moment decisions in certain situations, such as emergencies, but you simply cannot allow impulsive decisions to wreak havoc on your future. In most matters, taking the time to respond rather than react could pay huge dividends.

We finally have a simple, concise guide to assist young and old alike in how to make good decisions. This guide will help you realize that all decisions have possible solutions that don't always have to be emotional. Using this guide as a tool, you can evaluate your prospective decisions with more clarity and, I hope, achieve a better outcome.

For the Teen Reader: Why You Should Read Decisionology

During your childhood and adolescence, your parents and other adults have offered you choices of what you do or don't want—all you had to do was pick one or the other. Now, as a high-school student, you will increasingly be faced with decisions that require you to assess what options are available to you and decide which one is the best. This is a significant departure from the time when you had only to choose between option A and option B.

For example, you'll have to decide how you want to dress, with whom you want to hang out, what grades you want, and how willing you are to commit to a study program that will help you reach your goals. You'll have to decide which, if any, extracurricular activities to participate in. You'll also face decisions regarding personal hygiene and what type of first impression you hope to make.

This guide will provide you with some tools that will aid your decision-making processes. It will explain many of the different types of decisions and help you find a starting point in the process of evaluating which decision is right for you. I hope this guide will assist you in choosing a course of action or coming to a decision by giving you some simple insights into how you might approach your decision making. Periodically, "You Make the Call" questions will give you the opportunity to exercise your decision-making skills in real-life situations. I use the word "exercise" because these questions may well require you to utilize your decision-making skills in brand-new ways. If you use only one of the tools in this guide to make a better life-changing decision, you have triumphed!

Decision making is one of the most important aspects of your maturation process. How you make decisions, as well as the decisions themselves, has a critical impact on both your future and the lives of others. These decisions weave the fabric of the person you will ultimately become, and your adult self will be shaped by the decision-making process you begin utilizing as an adolescent. More precisely, you are growing up, and good decisions will help you become a responsible adult!

A Life-Changing Decision

I was sixteen years old, enjoying a gorgeous, hot summer day in the Big Hole Valley of Montana with three of my closest friends. We'd traveled to a local hot-spring swimming facility—a great place to have some fun and let off some steam. A lot of people were in the pool when we arrived, and we proceeded to have a good time, diving and playing with beach balls. I was in the shallow end, which was three or four feet deep, with a couple of my friends when one of my friends noticed something purple at the bottom of the pool, close to where we were standing. He asked us what we thought it was. We didn't have a clue, so he dove under the water. A few seconds later, he stood up with his arms outstretched, holding what looked like a three- or four-year-old boy, who was purple and definitely not breathing. Clearly, we believed, the boy had drowned; but we immediately decided that we should get help to see if he could be revived. Luck was on the little guy's side. The high-school basketball coach from Anaconda, where we all went to school, happened to be in the lobby, and he rushed to the boy's side and began efforts to resuscitate him. After what seemed like ten minutes of intensive effort, the coach was able to revive him—even today I think this was truly a miracle. This decision to go for help immediately illustrates how quickly a life can be changed forever in a very short time.

Consequences of a Bad Decision

Four high-school senior boys were enjoying their senior reception. After a short discussion, they decided to leave the reception and head to a nearby town where they could get served alcohol in a bar. After drinking for a couple of hours, they decided to drive to another nearby town, even though they were all clearly drunk. On their way home after three o'clock in the morning, the driver fell asleep at the wheel. He was going approximately seventy miles per hour and failed to make a left turn at an intersection. The vehicle went airborne and rolled several times; the car was totaled and three of the four boys were severely injured. Two of the injured boys were able to recover after extensive rehabilitation and medical assistance. One of the boys, who'd had a brilliant future in art ahead of him, incurred a devastating injury that completely prevented him from ever realizing his dreams. He was confined to a wheelchair for years and suffered significant physical disabilities that changed his life and the lives of his family members forever.

The decisions these boys made, which violated the law on several levels, were made without a lot of forethought regarding right or wrong or potential consequences. They were concerned only with having a good time, and they felt immune from getting caught or being involved in a horrendous accident.

The ability to make decisions is not only important but also essential in the life of every human being. Young people face decisions on a daily basis, from the very moment they become aware that more than one course of action is available.

Schools do a good job of teaching young people information, facts, skill sets, and much more. Our educators should be praised and honored for the job that they perform. Your teachers have provided you with the skills necessary to read, study, analyze, and pursue many of life's challenges. It is your job to utilize to the fullest all of the learning experiences and skills you have gained to make the very finest decisions possible. Your ability to make the best decisions no matter what challenges you face will be one of the primary factors determining your success or failure in life.

Simple versus Complex Decisions

Simple decisions are just that: simple. Some examples are to brush or not brush your teeth daily, or to do or not do your homework. In both examples, the decision is ultimately yours; but right away we see that even simple decisions can carry negative consequences if the right decision is not made. Simple decisions seem to require very little thought and are often made with almost no consideration of the consequences. But it is important to realize that even a simple decision can have significant consequences; never assume that a simple decision is not an important decision. Even though you can make a simple decision by deciding either yes or no, don't allow yourself to fall into a habit of thinking that simple decisions can't have negative end results that may very well affect your life—if not now, possibly at a later time. A good way to decide whether a simple decision is an important decision is to try to mentally list the decision's potential consequences. If you come up with a list of significant consequences for your simple decision, there is a good chance that it is also an important decision.

Not brushing your teeth is a simple decision with serious negative consequences over the long term; you will leave yourself vulnerable to cavities and damage your future social opportunities with an unattractive smile caused by unsightly teeth. When you don't do your homework, you have made a simple decision that can have both immediate and long-term consequences. Your teachers will ultimately have to give you a failing grade if you can't pass the tests; and, if you get enough failing grades, your future career opportunities will be severely limited.

Learn to ask yourself this question prior to making any simple or not-so-simple decisions: How will this decision impact my life as well as the lives of others? You'll find that by training yourself to have this simple self-discussion, you'll often make a much better decision for yourself as well as others.

Unlike a simple decision, a complex decision involves many variables and factors that must be thoroughly analyzed and weighed accordingly. You'll often realize immediately that to make the best decision, you'll need to do research or even request others' assistance. Another fact that may become immediately apparent is that this complex decision may require a significant amount of time to consider. Some examples of complex decisions are how to deal with a bully; how to say no to drugs; which college, community college, or trade school to attend; or which branch of the military to join. You may face the question of whether or not to keep a secret that you know will protect someone but potentially hurt someone else. You may wonder if asking for a math tutor to keep you from failing will make you look dumb in your friend's eyes. A few of these examples are explained in greater depth in the sections that follow.

How to Deal with a Bully

You're confronted daily by a school bully who has made your life a living hell, and you've decided to come forward and tell your parents. You've been very reluctant to tell anyone, fearing even more harassment, but you've finally had enough. You've been beaten up and mentally harassed for the past six months before class, during lunch, and even through text messages at night. You know you're doing the right thing but are aware that this action will potentially involve several parties, including the bully, the parents of the bully, your parents, the school principal, maybe the police, and maybe even your friends. Again, you're doing the right thing, but resolving this situation may involve many individuals and the collection of information. This is the type of decision that will take some time to consider, but your life should be much better because of it. You have rights as a human being, and by making a decision to come forward, you're taking a positive step toward stopping this terrible behavior.

How to Say No to Drugs

The more complex the decision, the more time you'd hope to have to make it. In life, however, this isn't always the case—you may be faced with a tough, complex decision and have only a short time period to address it. For example, you're with a close friend, heading to a house party, when he pulls the car into a vacant lot and stops the engine. He says he's decided to try a new drug that's been circulating around school, and he offers you some of his supply. You've never tried drugs of any kind and don't want to start now. But he's your close friend, and his approval is very important to you. You feel that if you don't participate, your friend will think less of you and your friendship may be in jeopardy. Of course, he's expecting you to join in immediately. You've had the drug talk with your parents and swore you've never done drugs and never will. You don't want to let your parents down, but, more than that, you know in your heart you're not interested in becoming a druggie. The decision time is now. You have to make this complex decision, which has so many variables and could affect the rest of your life, right now. After quickly assessing all the variables in front of you, your decision is to decline your friend's invitation and vote your conscience. Sometimes in life even complex decisions have simple answers.

In different situations where you feel you need more time to make the right decision, ask if you can be given more time, if possible. In rare cases, you may have to pass the decision process on to someone who has more time to research the right answers or who is more qualified to render a decision. But remember—I said this is rare!

Which College, Trade School, or Military Branch to Choose

When choosing a college, trade school, or military branch, you must base your initial decision (an emotional decision) on your own personal preferences—in other words, you have to feel that it would be a good decision for you. But this is just a starting point. Even if your initial decision feels like a good fit emotionally, before you make a final decision, you must examine the specific details and variables involved, which will require a great deal of research. You'll need to ask yourself practical questions: Is this school or military option a good fit financially for you and, possibly, your parents? How much financial aid will you need? How about eligibility—do you or can you qualify for admission? When will you have to make your final decision and send in your formal application? Have you taken your college-entrance admission tests yet? How are your high-school grades? When do you intend to discuss your intentions with your parents? These are just a few of the questions you'll need to answer.

Whether to Keep a Harmful Secret

When deciding whether to keep a secret that will protect someone but potentially hurt others, you must evaluate the pros and cons (the good versus the bad) to determine a course of action. For example, your best friend has told you in strict confidence that she is secretly seeing the boyfriend of another close friend. On the surface, you may feel that you must keep the secret, because doing so will ensure that you'll remain your friend's confidant, which is very important to you. However, in cases like this, you must be willing to dig deeper and decide whether maintaining your silence could bring adverse consequences. If you decide to keep the secret, won't the close friend feel betrayed if she finds out that you knew about the cheating boyfriend all along and chose not to tell her? Will you lose your close friend if she finds out you chose not to reveal this secret? Will deciding to keep this secret cause you to feel uneasy or deceptive around your close friend? Answering these questions is not easy, but a good decision maker must be willing to do it. Don't just look for the easy way out. Beyond the basic decision of whether to keep the secret, you must decide if you're willing to risk others getting hurt. Are you going to feel guilty for not coming forward? In a different type of situation, is this something that should be discussed with a person of authority, such as the police? Always remember that whenever it is a matter of legality, you have an obligation to come forward to the authorities as soon as possible.

Whether to Ask for a Math Tutor

Deciding to ask for help from a math tutor is a complex decision, possibly because it involves admitting to someone else that you need assistance. Also, when you ask for help, you may feel that you are incapable of doing math problems that others are handling just fine. You also may have to decide with whom to discuss the issue first—your parents or your math teacher. Your decision may also involve the potential for feeling embarrassed in front of your peers. You should realize that the decision to ask for a math tutor is a mature decision that has a gigantic payoff; it will be applauded by the people who really matter in your life. Furthermore, you have nothing to be embarrassed about; your tutor may simply need to explain some of the terms and show you how to work the problems at a slower pace. Never allow yourself to be embarrassed for deciding to ask for help. And never forget that any decision that ultimately helps you improve will always be viewed by anybody with a good head on his or her shoulders as the right decision—no exceptions!

To summarize, we have so far discussed the two basic types of decisions: simple decisions and complex decisions. From this point forward, we will discuss many of the different decisions, various aspects of decision making, and simple tools you'll need to assist you in making some of your life decisions.

You Make the Call

1. What is a simple decision that you make every day?
2. What decisions do you make on your own?
3. Do you enjoy making decisions that affect your everyday life?
4. Do you ask for assistance from others when making a tough decision?

Short-Term versus
Long-Term Decisions

An important question to ask yourself is whether the decision you're facing will make a difference just for today (short term), or if it will have an ongoing impact on your future for many years to come (long term). If your answer is that the decision will have a long-term effect on your life or the lives of others, you'll want to be sure to thoroughly analyze all the variables before reaching a final decision.

Many times we find ourselves reaching for quick-fix or temporary decisions, which are designed only to satisfy our desire for instant gratification. Sometimes these quick-fix decisions are exactly what are called for at the time. For example, when you need a short-term energy boost, maybe you decide to eat a candy bar at two thirty in the afternoon to get you through to dinner at five. The consequence of your decision is fairly immediate: a short-term feeling of satisfaction in both your stomach and your brain.

But often we find ourselves seeking out quick-fix/temporary decisions when we should be looking further down the road and deciding on more mature solutions. For example, when you are supposed to thoroughly read and study a chapter in your textbook for your homework assignment, perhaps you decide instead to briefly skim the material and hope to fool your teacher. Here you've made a quick-fix decision that can have an immediate negative impact if your teacher calls on you and you are unprepared to answer her questions. If you make a habit of skimming instead of thoroughly reading your homework assignments, the consequences could be devastating. Not only will you suffer when you have to take the final, but you'll be in trouble later on when you have to move on to more difficult courses and you haven't learned the proper foundation material.

Questions to Ask Yourself

It is very important to ask yourself a few basic questions before considering a decision in the first place. Good questions to ask are the following: Will I feel good afterward if I make this decision now? Is this decision going to hurt others or me? Do I have to make this decision right now, or can it wait until tomorrow? Should I ask my parents before making this decision? Will I get into trouble if I make this decision? Will making this decision break the law in any way? Is this a smart decision to be making at this time? Is this my decision to make in the first place? It's possible that you are not the right person to make the decision in the first place. In some cases, maybe somebody else, perhaps someone in another class or with more experience, should be making this decision. Sometimes circumstances may present you with a decision that you realize is beyond your current ability or level of sophistication. You must be ready to express this to your teacher, parent, or whoever is in charge of the decision in question.

Focus and Objective Decision Questions

Some excellent questions to ask before committing to a decision are the following: What is my objective? What do I want to accomplish by making this decision? You'll find that if you clearly define your objective or objectives, your focus and ultimate decision will be, more often than not, a better or sounder decision.

You Make the Call

1. Will making this decision be good for me as well as others? Think of a decision you made where you asked or should have asked yourself this question.
2. Think of a decision you made where you should have taken more time to think before you acted.
3. List five quick-fix decisions you've made this week.
4. Discuss the consequences of one of your quick-fix decisions.

Consequences

The education, learning, and life experiences you've encountered in your lifetime will largely determine the decisions that you make and the consequences resulting from your actions. Before making a decision, you should always make a conscientious effort to apply your education and life experiences in order to arrive at a decision that you feel in your heart is the best one. You must do your very best to be aware of the potential consequences before making any decisions that could hurt others, yourself, or the environment.

Consequences come in all shapes and sizes. Some are good, some are bad, and some may make us wish for another chance to make a better decision. For example, perhaps you decided your freshman year to volunteer at the local hospital for two hours after school on Mondays, Wednesdays, and Fridays. Now, after four years of volunteering, you feel certain that your career will deal, in some way, with medicine. The consequences of your decision to volunteer have had a very positive influence on your future line of work.

Consider two more examples. First, perhaps you chose Spanish as an elective in high school and found out that you really enjoy it. You've made some great friends thanks to your original decision, and you also have the advantage of speaking a language that has become a very significant part of American culture. Second, perhaps you decided to take as many computer courses in high school as you could. Now, after you've studied computers for four years, your friends and your parents often come to you for advice, which makes you feel great and gives you a real sense of pride in your skills and accomplishments.

In a different vein, perhaps you decided in your sophomore year that if you did just enough to get by in your studies, then you'd have a lot more time to have fun and goof off with your friends. Now you're coming to the end of your junior year, and you realize that you haven't prepared yourself for college, which is where most of your good friends are headed. Your decision to goof off and just get by in your studies has consequences, and now you know that it's very unlikely that you can pass the college entrance exams.

In another situation, maybe you passed your driver's test with flying colors, and, the following Saturday, you got permission to use your parents' car to go to a movie with your friends. You decided to show off for your friends after the movie and ended up getting a speeding ticket for going fifty-five miles per hour in a thirty-five-miles-per-hour zone. Your decision to speed and break the law had consequences that cost you in a variety of ways. You lost your driving privileges until your parents could once again have you covered on their automobile insurance, and you damaged the strong bond of trust and integrity you had established previously with your parents. These are serious consequences. You can't rebuild trust and confidence with your parents overnight—it takes time and effort on your part.

The consequences of your decisions can range from insignificant to totally life changing, in both negative and positive ways. For instance, maybe your mother asks you if you've cleaned up your bedroom, and you decide to lie and say yes even though you haven't done any cleaning whatsoever. When your mother checks your room later and realizes that you lied, she revokes your allowance for a week. In this example, the consequences are fairly insignificant, and you'll live to see another day. In a totally different example, perhaps you decide to organize a fund drive at your school to help the family of one of your fellow students, who has recently lost her home to a fire that destroyed the entire uninsured home and all of her family's belongings. Your decision resulted in raising $450 from the students and teachers and was cited by one of the parents as his primary motivation for organizing a citywide fund drive that brought in over $11,000. The consequences of your initial decision to start a fund drive in your high school were that a fellow student and her family received support during their time of need. Your fund drive was the driving force behind the parent's fund-raising efforts, and your name was mentioned in an article about the fire, giving you recognition for your efforts. The consequences of your initial fund-raising effort ultimately affected an entire city in a very positive way.

In another situation, perhaps you've chosen to swim in the ocean in an area where there are known riptide hazards. You're a good swimmer and feel confident that you can handle yourself in the water. After you decided to go swimming in this particular area, you talked one of your friends into joining you, against his better judgment. You'd been swimming for only a short time when both of you were caught in a riptide. After struggling in the water for over forty-five minutes, you both finally made it back to the beach, totally exhausted and lucky to be alive. The consequences of your poor decision: you lost a good friend, who says he'll never do anything with you again. You are now very reluctant to even consider going swimming in the ocean. On the more positive side, you've developed a more realistic, mature view of the risks associated with swimming in the ocean, which is a good thing. You are now fully aware that your stupid decision to swim in a dangerous area came terrifyingly close to killing both you and your friend. You realize more than ever that you are not invincible and that your decisions can have a huge impact on your life as well as the lives of others.

The many different consequences resulting from your decisions could easily vary from happiness and jubilation to sadness to extreme sorrow and regret. Regret can come in many different forms, and often it is the result of poor decision making. For example, consider a seventeen-year-old high-school student who has saved all his extra money for years to buy a motorcycle. The day finally arrives, and he buys a used motorcycle for $1,800. That summer, whenever he's not working, he spends all his free time riding and racing around town. He learns to do wheelies and other stunts and really gets into driving at high speeds. He is going over eighty miles per hour on a secondary highway one day when he loses control. He is thrown more than 150 feet through the air; after he crashes to the ground, he continues to slide and rip his body in every way imaginable. Remarkably, he survives, but he suffers severe physical disfigurements, including a broken back, broken legs, a broken arm, and a massive loss of skin, which has literally been scraped from his body. Today, the consequences of his decision to speed recklessly include the following: complete paralysis of both legs as well as both arms and the use of his hands, confinement to either bed or a wheelchair twenty-four hours per day, and the need for round the clock caretakers. It should go without saying that he has regretted his decision to speed since the day the accident happened.

Learn to ask yourself whether there is a strong possibility that you will regret your decision once you make your decision. If your answer is yes, then you probably should not make the decision in the first place. Poor decisions can result in consequences that can wreak havoc on your life as well as the lives of your family and loved ones. The consequences of bad decisions can plague you forever, as in the example of someone who decides to commit a crime and ends up in prison for life.

On the positive side of the ledger, good decisions translate into positive consequences that will make your life better and more fulfilling in many different ways. For example, maybe you decided in your freshman year of high school that you wanted to try out for the track team. You made the team freshman year, and, by the time you were a senior, you were one of the top sprinters in your school. Now your decision to join the track team has translated into a full-ride scholarship to college, and your parents couldn't be prouder of you. To put it in perspective, the decision you made as a fifteen-year-old freshman put you on a course that culminated in a track scholarship and a true sense of accomplishment. The consequences of your decision to go out for the track team translated into a tremendous, life-changing opportunity for you and your family.

In another example, perhaps you have allowed your hair to grow since the seventh grade, and it hangs to your waist. You're now heading into your sophomore year, and all your friends are constantly urging you to cut it. One month before heading back to school, you make the ultimate decision to get it cut short. It's a tough decision; your father loves your long hair, and you've occasionally gotten some nice compliments from others. You're really concerned about whether your decision is the right one and what your father will think. Your mother thinks it's a good idea and that the change will be good for you. Your mother arranges an appointment at her hair salon and goes with you on the big day. You and your mother can't believe how much different short hair makes you look. But the big questions still remain: What will your friends—especially the boys—think about the new you? And even more important—what will your father think?

The consequences of your decision to finally cut your hair are overwhelming. Your friends say it makes you look fabulous, and several boys have even complimented you on your new look. Maybe you're just imagining things, but it seems as if you're more popular with the guys as well as the girls. Best of all, your father says he really likes the new you and thinks you made the right decision. The icing on the cake is that you like the end result—you made a wise decision, and the consequences couldn't have turned out better!

You will find that many of the most jubilant, exhilarating times of your life are the direct result of good decisions and the resulting consequences. You will find that good decisions resulting in positive consequences are often a direct reflection of your ability to make sound decisions. Always remember that you are the one who makes it happen for you. You are the one who creates your destiny, largely by making good decisions that result in better consequences and outcomes for your future. Over time, the cumulative effect of sound decisions will likely translate into a successful life and a happier existence. So before you make a decision, it's critical to first make a habit of thinking before you act.

You Make the Call

1. List two good decisions you've made in the past six months.
2. List the consequences of the good decisions listed for the previous question.
3. List two bad decisions you've made in the past six months.
4. List the consequences of the bad decisions listed for the previous question.

Personal-Growth Decisions

A personal-growth decision will help you improve your life. Personal-growth decisions often require a bit of soul searching; sometimes you face the possibility of giving something up or significantly adjusting your daily life. But this adjustment will never come to pass unless you decide to grow in a very positive direction. You must ultimately choose the direction you want to travel in your life—and only you can make this choice. Life-changing personal-growth decisions will almost always provide benefits that you'd never thought about at the time. This type of decision can carry with it various added benefits that you'd never even considered when making your original decision. Whenever you decide to pursue personal growth as opposed to remaining at your present level of accomplishment, you'll almost always thank yourself later.

Joining the Debate Team

The decision of whether to join the debate team is an example of a personal-growth decision. Joining the team will require you to budget your time more carefully and improve your public-speaking abilities, both of which will assist you in many of your future endeavors. There are other benefits as well; for example, you may develop new friends whom you may never have met otherwise. Also, the public-speaking skills you develop could help you immeasurably in your English class when you're required to give a speech or when you're asked to speak at a social event or in other impromptu situations.

Other Examples of Personal-Growth Decisions

Another example of a personal-growth decision is deciding to improve your vocabulary by learning the spelling and definition of one new word each week for an entire year. If you set aside just fifteen or thirty minutes each week, by the end of one year you'll have increased your vocabulary by fifty-two new words. This would be a great decision, and you'll find that, very often, successful people have a rich vocabulary that they began developing when they were young students.

In a different vein entirely, consider deciding to declare war on junk food. Swear off eating at least one specific kind of junk food, like candy, for the next three months, or whatever time period you feel comfortable with. The consequences of your decision will be good for your body and may even help improve your complexion. You'll also have extra money to use elsewhere. Best of all, depending on how much you were eating previously, you may lose a few pounds. This truly could be a win–win situation for your self-control, your budget, and your physical well-being!

Another good idea is to decide to learn how to prepare and serve one complete evening meal for your family. This is a personal-growth decision that you'll be able to use for the rest of your life. Since your parents likely have a lot of meal-preparation experience, you may want to consult them for menu advice. Or you may want to do your own research and surprise the whole family some evening. You'll find that the knowledge and skills you learn from making this personal-growth decision will be ready and waiting throughout your life. Sooner or later, you'll find yourself in a situation in which you'll have to cook for yourself or others. Deciding to learn how to prepare a meal and, ultimately, enjoy the food you prepared may easily be one of the best personal-growth decisions you ever make.

Risk versus Reward

Will the reward be worth the risk you're contemplating? Is the risk too high compared to what you'll receive in return? Consider this good example: You're a seventeen-year-old boy and have been dating the same fifteen-year-old girl for three months. Sometime soon, you'll have to decide how you are going to handle the possibility of a sexual relationship. Your parents have told you that sex is absolutely not acceptable during high school. Your school has a strict code of conduct that specifically spells out that this is not an option while you're in high school. You also know that sex brings several huge risks, including the following: pregnancy; sexually transmitted diseases (STDs); the charge of statutory rape if one partner is a minor, which could lead to a prison term, probation, and/or possible expulsion from school; faulty or ineffective condoms, which could lead to pregnancy or an STD; and violation of the oath you made to your parents that you would not have sex during high school. The reward for these and other risks is physical sexual gratification, which will be gone in a very short period of time. Your desire to satisfy your sexual urges may lead you to make a decision that could have a massive impact on your entire future. In this example, the risks definitely outweigh the reward. You should always be willing to make decisions regarding risky behavior only after carefully considering the risks. In this example, the proper decision is to wait to have sex.

In a different scenario, perhaps your fourteen-year-old friend just called and wants to pick you up in her dad's car and head to her boyfriend's house party, ten miles out of town. You'd really like to go, but you know she doesn't have her license yet, so she'd be driving illegally. You'd also have to lie to your parents about going to a friend's house for the evening, because they're very aware that your friend isn't old enough to drive. What also concerns you is that your friend told you that her boyfriend's father always leaves his liquor cabinet open, so there's a good chance your underage pal will be driving home under the influence of alcohol, probably after one in the morning. Your decision to get in a car with a drunk, underage driver brings several risks. First, it's illegal, and if your friend gets pulled over by the police, you'll be taken to the police station along with her. It's also dangerous to put your life in the hands of a fourteen-year-old who is not certified as a licensed driver in your state. It's also extremely risky—and illegal—to mix alcohol with driving. If your friend wrecks her dad's car or gets into an accident, chances are that you both could be injured or worse. Finally, let's not lose sight of the fact that you had to lie to your parents; this decision brings the very real possibility that you may get caught and destroy their trust and your credibility.

Now let's look at the rewards for deciding to go to this house party with your friend. You get the opportunity to hang out with your friends and maybe get drunk. You may get to meet some new kids and make some new friends. Now, ask yourself this: Are a few hours of friendship and partying worth all the risks involved?

You Make the Call

1. List and discuss two of the hardest decisions you've ever had to make.
2. Explain how you were ultimately able to make the decisions listed above and if you needed or asked for assistance.
3. List the consequences of these decisions that affected you the most. What lessons did you learn?
4. List the consequences of these decisions that affected others.

The Prudent-Student Test

A great tool to use when faced with a decision like the one in the previous chapter is the Prudent-Student Test. This test essentially asks, "What would a smart student do if he or she were presented with the same decision you're contemplating, but if he or she had all of the facts but none of the personal conflicts to cloud his or her judgment?" In other words, pretend a classmate whose judgment you greatly respect must make the same decision you're struggling with. You can provide this student with all the information you have and see if your final decision differs from his or hers. The prudent student may be able to make a better decision than you, because his or her judgment is not clouded by the emotions that may prevent you from coming to a realistic decision. Ultimately, of course, the final decision is yours.

Here's another example. Maybe your best friend broke up with his girlfriend six weeks ago, and now you'd really like to hang out with her. You're torn between your allegiance to your friend and your desire to go out with his ex. You decide to see whether a prudent student would decide to go out with his best friend's ex-girlfriend, so you give him all the details about your friendship and other relevant information. Your tentative decision to go out with her is just the opposite of what the prudent student decides. Your analysis reveals that your best friend would be offended by your decision and might very well terminate your friendship. The Prudent-Student Test also indicates that your five-year friendship with your best friend is not something that you should be willing to risk for a relationship that may never come to pass. In this situation, you've used the Prudent-Student Test to see how your final decision compares with the decision made by a prudent student. You may find that the more objective you are when conducting your Prudent-Student Test, the more realistic and helpful your end results.

Domino Decisions

Be very cautious when making a decision that will require you to make a second decision and possibly several more decisions in the future. For example, a decision to buy a $1,000 car that is twenty-five years old and in rough shape mechanically will almost assuredly necessitate future decisions to pay for repairs that could cost more than the car itself. Potential upkeep and repairs may include new tires ($200 to $400), a tune-up ($150 to $400), new brakes ($200 to $400), a new battery ($100), and so on. Each one of these items will require another decision that originates from your original decision to buy a cheap car. It should be noted that buying a cheap car may well be an acceptable decision, as long as you're aware that doing so may bring a hidden set of additional costs and future decisions. It is also important to realize that this type of domino-decision situation may involve your own or others' safety. You'll have to fork over payments for repairs unless you decide to leave the car parked and avoid potentially life-threatening hazards. For example, bad brakes must be fixed—the car can't be driven safely without a good braking system. Your decision is, simply, fix the brakes or park the car. So your original decision dominoed into multiple costly decisions, as well as decisions that must be made regarding safety. The moral of this story is that a domino decision hastily made today can translate into multiple costly decisions down the road. Always try to decide what the real costs will ultimately be for any decision.

Consider another example of a domino decision. During the summer before your junior year, perhaps you met a student you really like but who happens to be a senior at your school. You both really enjoy the other's company, and you decide that just because there's a year difference in age between you, there's no reason why you shouldn't hang out together at school and after school. This initial decision now requires you to decide how you're going to hang out with your existing friends, who are all juniors, and your new senior friend. Your junior friends have an attitude toward upperclassmen that makes it pretty clear that juniors should hang out only with juniors. Your initial decision to hang out with your senior friend may cause a rift between you and your junior friends, which you don't want. You must also decide how to fit into your senior friend's clique of friends; you're unsure whether they'll accept you into their circle. You may also be faced with having your junior classmates not accept your decision to spend time with upperclassmen. Your original domino decision may ultimately require you to choose between hanging out with your original circle of friends and your new senior friend. You may have to decide how to juggle your time and activities with your senior friend and your junior friends. Your original domino decision has set off a chain reaction that will require you to make several other tough decisions. Note, however, that as long as you're aware of the potential future decisions that usually come with a domino decision, this decision is not necessarily wrong or inappropriate. Just be sure you're in a position to handle whatever the future decisions may entail and not harm others in the process.

You Make the Call

1. List a domino decision that you've made in your lifetime.
2. What were the subsequent decisions that arose from the original decision?

Decisions with Legal Consequences

You decide to exceed the speed limit. This kind of impulsive decision can bring consequences that can wreck your life and the lives of others in your car, as well as innocent people in other vehicles. When you get pulled over by the police, you risk being fined, having your license suspended, and possibly serving time in jail. Note that I said "when," not "if," you get pulled over. If you're the one whose speeding led to a horrendous accident, your life as you once knew it may well be over. You should always have the answer when it comes to decisions regarding breaking the law: a definitive no is always the right answer!

No Decision Is Still a Decision

Always keep in mind that when you decide *not* to make a decision, you've still made a decision. In some cases, there may be consequences for your failure to act or decide.

Consider this example of failing to make a decision. Perhaps your biology teacher has asked you to help clean up after the annual Christmas party being held in the school gym. She tells you to be at the gym the following Saturday at one o'clock with nine other students and to wear old clothes. You completely ignore the one o'clock deadline and choose to go skiing with your friends instead. Your failure to show up and help with the cleanup is still a decision, and it has consequences that affect not only you but others as well. You have demonstrated to your biology teacher that you can't be depended upon to keep your word; many would consider this a matter of not being accountable. The fact that you decided not to help out also affected the others who had to take your place and do more work. The lesson here is obvious: inactivity, failure to act, or failure to come to a decision to act can have far-reaching implications. You should always be willing to take the time to evaluate the potential consequences of your indecision or failure to act. Then, if you decide to ignore an impending deadline or fail to act, you have at least based your decision on a responsible approach and an awareness of potential fallout.

Some Decision Is Better Than No Decision

Keep in mind that, many times, some decision—any decision—is better than no decision at all. You just have to be aware that a nondecision often can and will result in a positive or negative outcome. Don't fall for the rule of thumb that any decision is *always* better than no decision. This is true only in some cases. Note that you should do your very best to research and thoroughly explore any potential decision that you're considering not making before you take that approach. Don't allow yourself to fall into a habit of not making decisions, period. Once you have adequately considered the decision in question and you feel justified in your research, then you can consider a nondecision approach.

Consider this example of a situation in which some decision is better than no decision at all. Perhaps you've just received your high-school diploma, and your choices for your future are going to college, attending a trade school, or joining the military. You ultimately make no choice regarding your future; instead, you allow the winds of time to make the decision for you. Your failure to make a decision that would have, most assuredly, improved your future job prospects and earning ability may well haunt you for the rest of your life. Your future will now be dictated by whatever jobs you can find that require no specialized knowledge or training. Generally speaking, this means you'll be able to apply only for jobs that pay minimum wage and often bring no fringe benefits. Your failure to make some decision after high-school graduation has now placed you at the very bottom of the earning pool. You'll find it very difficult to obtain even the basics of life, such as food, rent, and utilities, on a minimum-wage salary.

On the other hand, had you decided to improve your bargaining position with specialized knowledge and training in the military or at a college or trade school, you would have positioned yourself for much higher earning potential. You would have had a much wider choice of opportunities, occupationally as well as financially. Your future would not have been limited to whatever minimum-wage jobs were available. (Note that there is nothing wrong with minimum-wage jobs when you're looking for your first job. And when you're still in high school, most entry-level jobs pay minimum wage. The point is that ideally you'll use the entry-level position to move forward into a higher-paying position or job in the future.) Make no mistake: your financial well-being will largely dictate your future decisions in many areas of your life. You'll find that the majority of people who are doing well financially made the decision when they were younger to invest in their futures. A very strong case can be made for the fact that better decisions translate into more opportunities and a more successful life.

You Make the Call

1. List two situations in which you chose not to make a decision and discuss what prompted you to refrain from making a decision.

2. What were the consequences for you of not making a decision?

3. What were the consequences for other people of not making a decision?

4. What would you do differently if you were faced with the same decisions today?

5. At the time that you chose not to decide or to take any action, did you realize that, in effect, you were still making a decision not to act and that this might result in consequences?

6. Explain why making a habit of not making decisions is not a good idea.

Emotional Decisions

Decisions which you make based solely on your' emotions, have the potential to be extremely intense and very powerful. When you allow your emotions such as love, hate, or revenge to make your decisions, you are creating outcomes that have the potential to be very negative or positive. When you allow your emotions to override your ability to reason and think properly, it is your emotions that are truly making the decisions. We all make emotional decisions, and, ideally, we find that our outcomes are more positive than negative. When you're faced with an overwhelmingly negative emotion, allow yourself some time to think before you act, if at all possible. Of course, some emotional decisions just feel right; it's not a matter of thinking or pondering the pros and cons. For example, when we pass a water fountain, almost without thinking we stop to drink; or we compliment someone on a great outfit the minute we set eyes on him or her.

An example of a negative emotional decision is seeking revenge when you have been injured or humiliated by others. You want to even the score and possibly cause those responsible to feel the same pain, humiliation, and loss they made you feel. *Stop!* This negative and potentially dangerous thought process will most often lead to disastrous end results. A decision followed by vengeful actions cannot be reversed. This type of decision, which is powered by strong emotions, can wreck your and others' lives and future well-being.

Consider this example. Perhaps you find out that one of your close friends has been secretly hanging out with your boyfriend. She confesses that it's been going on for months, and she doesn't intend to stop seeing him. You're really angry, and your almost immediate emotional decision is to seek revenge and hurt both her and your boyfriend as much as they have hurt you. This would be a bad emotional decision on your part. You're totally justified in feeling betrayed and hurt, but you must force yourself to do everything in your power to not make an emotional decision to seek revenge. You must do your best to recognize that your immediate reaction is powered solely by emotion and that any decision you make in the moment will have the potential to hurt you as well as others. The consequences of an emotional decision to seek revenge could wreck your entire future and the lives of others. Do yourself a huge favor and allow yourself to cool down; then make the best rational decision you can in this emotionally charged situation. This is not an easy thing to do, but a levelheaded decision in this situation will almost always be the right decision.

Consider this much different example of a good emotional decision. Maybe you're in chemistry class, and your teacher is discussing the various forms of matter. He points out that our nation's highways are the unwanted recipients of a tremendous amount of discarded man-made matter every day. He surprises the class by asking for fifteen students to volunteer for a highway-cleansing project that aims to clean up a five-mile stretch of a secondary highway near the high school. You are so moved by your teacher's discussion that your emotions take over and you make an emotional decision to volunteer. In this example, your positive emotions were responsible for making a positive emotional decision, which you were able to arrive at almost without thinking.

In another example of a good emotional decision, you're selling your car for $2,000, and your best friend has been saving for his own car since he was a freshman; however, he has only $1,500 saved. You know in your heart that he would do anything for you, so you decide to sell your car to him for $1,500. You don't need any time at all to make this great emotional decision. This decision also qualifies as a feel-good decision. You've just made one of the better decisions of your young life. You helped someone near and dear to you, and, in the process, you've helped yourself feel better about who you are.

Leaving the Scene of an Emotional Decision

When you find yourself confronted with a highly charged emotional decision with a strong potential for negative consequences or bad results, you should determine whether the situation will allow you to remove yourself from the scene. You may need a good deal of emotional control and restraint to avoid an immediate emotional reaction or decision. If you can go somewhere else, where you can settle your nerves and try to reach a more responsible decision, you'll give yourself a far better chance of a more positive outcome. Once again, this will require a great deal of emotional control, but if you can discipline yourself emotionally to refrain from an immediate reaction, you may be able to make a better decision. Note that your emotions can sometimes be your best protection, such as an emotional decision based on fear to avoid swimming in turbulent water. You have to figure out for yourself when you can and should trust your emotions when making an emotional decision, and be guided accordingly.

Emotional Decisions: A Conclusion

Sometimes you'll do the right thing by going with your heart and making an emotional decision. Other times, you'll need to evaluate right versus wrong—or negative versus positive—in terms of your decision's potential consequences, and act accordingly. Other times, you'll have to use your best judgment based on all the variables and utilize your education and experiences at home and in school, as well as your views on life, to make an informed decision.

The Feel-Good Decision Test

Some great questions to ask before making a final decision are the following: How will this decision make me feel after I have committed myself to a course of action? Will I feel a sense of pride, jubilation, happiness, sadness, remorse, or regret? Will I want to take it back if I could? Before applying this feel-good decision test, you should have taken the time to adequately look at all of the other criteria involved in making the decision. Once you feel that you have done your best to view your prospective decision from various angles, you then can apply the feel-good test to your decision. It should go without saying that this does not apply to irresponsible and unacceptable behavior, such as secretly getting high at school, just because the decision will make you feel good. You should also realize that just because you think your decision will make you feel good, it's entirely possible that others may not be pleased with your decision. An obvious example is a sporting contest, where your decision to make a winning play will definitely cause some hurt feelings on the losing team. In this example, you should make decisions that are designed to win the game—you know in advance of your decision that the end result will cause some bruised egos.

Consider this example of a feel-good decision. Perhaps you must decide between hanging out with your friends and studying for your geometry final, which is scheduled for tomorrow. You're torn between what will make you feel good right now—hanging out with your friends—and what will feel good in the long term. You have to decide if immediate gratification in the form of hanging out with your friends for the next three hours will feel better than the potential high grade that you'll receive on your geometry final if you study, which will end up on your permanent high-school transcript. Your final decision is between immediate, short-term pleasure and a potentially high grade on your final, which will last for the rest of your life. In this situation, you can ask yourself these simple feel-good questions: How will I feel after my geometry test tomorrow if I don't study for it this evening? Will I feel regret or remorse for choosing to hang out with my friends? Will receiving a low or failing grade on my test be worth spending a few hours with my friends? How much better will I feel if I decide to take a pass on hanging out with my friends and choose to use the time to study? Which decision will make me feel better about myself tomorrow, next week, or at the end of the semester? Which decision do I feel in my heart is the right one?

By utilizing this kind of soul searching, you will often find that after you've answered your questions, your decision is obvious. You will have chosen what makes you feel good not only for today but for the tomorrows of your life as well.

You Make the Call

1. List three decisions you've made in the past six months where your final decision relied on the feel-good decision test.
2. Discuss the end results and consequences of these decisions.

3. What have you learned about applying the feel-good decision test to your decision-making processes?
4. List one example of a decision you made in the last month where you had to choose between short-term gratification and long-term benefit. Discuss the details.

Time Is Your Ally

When you're faced with an important decision, take the time to think, analyze, and evaluate all the variables carefully before coming to your final decision. This is critical. When you have the time to make a proper decision, by all means use it to your fullest advantage. For instance, when you are told that your American history final will be on a Friday two weeks from now, you have plenty of time to decide on a study plan and prepare accordingly. On the other hand, when your teacher tells you at the beginning of class that there will be a pop quiz in a half hour and you have exactly twenty-five minutes to look over the past two chapters and prepare, you have to make some snap decisions on what to study and what not to study. You don't have enough time to study both chapters, so you have to decide what's most important—and you have to make this decision almost immediately so you can begin your review. This is a snap decision, or, more specifically, a decision you must make almost immediately. The time frame requires you to make a quick decision; your choice of study material might be much different if you were allowed adequate time to decide what topics you should focus on. Don't make snap decisions when you're deciding between life-changing alternatives or when you're given adequate time to properly evaluate the situation. Whenever you make decisions on the spur of the moment without taking the proper amount of time, you'll find that, most of the time, the outcomes could have been much better if only you'd slowed down a little bit.

Of course, occasionally we all face decisions that we have to make right now, without the time to seek others' opinions or feedback. In these situations, you'll just have to use your best judgment and hope for a positive result.

Learn to make time your friend and to use all the tools at your disposal to adequately analyze the variables involved to reach the best decision you can. Time will permit you to access others' ideas and solicit input from a divergent group of knowledgeable people. Be very careful to properly allocate your time for the decision process; otherwise, you might squander it and end up not having adequately utilized the gift of time that was given to you in the first place.

Consider this example of a decision where you utilize your amazing ally of time. Perhaps your English teacher has informed you in the first week of class that everyone will be required to read a novel of his or her choice and turn in a book report in six weeks. You have to make a decision that will allow you to take advantage of your greatest asset: time. Your decision should involve the creation of a schedule that includes a timetable allocating so many hours per day or per week to reading your novel. This timetable should specify the number of chapters you need to read on a weekly basis so that you can complete the project by the end of the six-week period. You also need to set up a method of monitoring your progress to make sure that you're on target and not falling behind. By properly using time and following your timetable, you should be well prepared when you begin writing your book report.

In the event that you fail to make a timely decision to utilize time, you will find that time will become your enemy the closer you get to the end of your course. Now you'll have to play catch-up by trying to squeeze more reading into a shorter period of time.

Daniel P. Gates

You would do well to develop the superb habit of always taking advantage of any allotment of time that you are given—this will pay huge dividends in your future!

You Make the Call

1. Discuss one decision you've made in your life where you used time as your ally in arriving at your final decision.

Being Decisive

The ability to make decisions based on available information is a good attribute to have in most cases. If you feel comfortable with the information available on a given topic and can render a quick decision, you will be praised by most people if the decision is correct, or at least the best decision available. Note that once you have all the pertinent information, you should be able to make your decision without delay. This is what is commonly referred to as being decisive. More specifically, when you face a decision regarding a subject or situation with which you are very familiar, you should be able to be decisive and make your decision readily. In this type of decision, you don't have to consult others or conduct research to locate the answers. You feel very confident that your decision is the right one. On the other hand, when you face a decision for which you don't know the answers, you should use your ally of time and do some research to obtain the information you need to render your decision. Once you've thoroughly researched your decision, you're in a position to be decisive without needing to delay your decision any further. Don't fall into the trap of trying to be decisive in a matter that will allow you plenty of time for thorough analysis, fact finding, and research. A thorough analysis will require you to look at your decision from all angles and possibly study and examine each to understand why or how they might affect your final decision.

Fact finding is the collection of any information relevant to your decision; such information can come from the library, the Internet, interviews with knowledgeable people (by phone or in person), and any other sources that may be helpful. (Your fact finding and research will be limited in high school but should become more important as you mature and face tough decisions in the future. The information is included here simply to provide a little insight into what your future decision-making processes may entail.) You need to take the time and make the effort to do research prior to making any important decision. You won't get a medal for being rapidly decisive in a matter that requires significant research and fact finding. More than likely, you'll be criticized for making a poor decision or, possibly, a costly mistake.

You Make the Call

1. List two decisive decisions you've made in the past six months.
2. What were the consequences of these decisions? How did you feel after making these decisions?

The Smart Student's Decision Tool

With pencil and paper, you can create a simple, effective decision tool like the one shown on the following page, which can assist you in your decision-making process. It provides you with a physical picture of the reasons for or against making a given decision and allows you to really focus on all the relevant variables involved. Your decision is usually going to fall on the side of the diagram that has the greatest number of reasons listed below it. However, some reasons will carry much more weight than others and outweigh multiple reasons on the opposite side of the diagram. Your good judgment will be the tool you use to ultimately make the decision.

REASONS FOR MAKING THE DECISION	REASONS AGAINST MAKING THE DECISION
Timing is right	Costs too much
Adequate information	Not safe
Will help others	It's illegal
Right course of action now	Not enough information
Parents agree it's the right decision	Parents think it's a bad idea
Highly recommended by a friend	Friend had very poor results
Research indicates it's a good decision	Need more time to study and fact find

Moral Decisions

A moral decision is right because you simply know in your heart and mind that it is the right course of action. You make your decision almost without having to think about it. This is possible thanks to many factors, not the least of which is your upbringing—how you've been taught by your parents and loved ones. Also responsible are your education and, possibly, your church, which may have provided you with a point of reference and a responsible code of conduct for many different aspects of life. You live your life according to a moral code of being kind to others and helping those less fortunate than you in their time of need. A good example here is assisting an elderly person who has fallen on the sidewalk in front of you and needs help getting back to his or her feet. You know instinctively and instantly that the right thing to do is give a helping hand. It's simply the right thing for you to do at that moment.

Another example of a moral decision is helping a wheelchair-bound individual open a door that does not have an automatic opening mechanism. Here again, your natural response is to step up and assist by opening the door. Your perspective, which you've gained from your life experiences, almost shouts at you to do the right thing now.

Consider one last example of a moral decision. Perhaps you're in town, hanging out with your friends, when you see a three-year-old girl, unattended, trying to cross a busy intersection all by herself. It's obvious that she's been separated from her mother or father and needs immediate assistance for safety's sake. You don't have to stop to consider whether you should step up and help her. Your moral upbringing and background tell you to immediately help this little girl in whatever way you can. Your personal moral code makes the decision for you.

These are only a few of the many different types of moral decisions that life presents us with on a daily basis. If you follow the rule to treat all human beings with respect, dignity, and kindness, your decision-making process when it comes to moral decisions will be nearly automatic.

Potential Advantages of Good Decision Making

Pride in the outcome and/or results	Helping others
Satisfaction in knowing you did it right	Self-confidence
Better test scores	Mental health
Better organization	Happiness
Personal growth	Physical well-being
Lasting friendships	Family cohesiveness
Graduation from high school, college, or trade school	Honorable military career
Peace of mind	Success in life

You Make the Call

1. List two moral decisions you've made in your lifetime.
2. What were the consequences of the moral decisions you listed for the first question?
3. To what or whom do you give credit for helping you make these moral decisions?

Personal Decisions

Personal decisions, such as deciding to spend time with one group of kids instead of another, are usually based on your innermost feelings and experiences. Other types of personal decisions, such as what clothes to wear, are often determined initially by your parents' budget as well as what your parents deem appropriate. These decisions affect you in a very personal way. As you can see, some personal decisions you make yourself, and others you make with the aid of your parents. Consider this example of a personal decision. Perhaps you've developed a big crush on a certain student, and you're dying to tell your best friend. You ultimately decide to tell your friend, but you make her swear to keep it a secret for now. You know you can trust her and that she'll always have your best interests at heart, so you feel your decision to tell her is safe. Special friends whose judgment you trust wholeheartedly are often a good choice if you need help with personal decisions.

Your parents may also be an excellent choice if you need help with personal decisions, depending on your comfort level with the types of decisions being discussed. For example, maybe you're having a minor problem with acne, and you really want to get rid of it as soon as possible. You decide to discuss it with your mother and ask her to help you find some type of treatment. You made a personal decision to discuss this very sensitive matter with a person you know will do her best to help you. In a different situation, perhaps you're contemplating getting your hair cut very short, just like the rest of the swim team, but you know your mother loves your long hair. You finally make a personal decision to discuss getting a very short haircut with your mother and hope for the best. You're pleasantly surprised when she says that now that you're seventeen years old, you're old enough to make your own personal decisions regarding how you want to cut your hair; nevertheless, she would still prefer that you keep it long.

Other times, you may be well served by spending some quiet time alone and doing some soul searching to find answers to the personal decisions you're facing. After you've had time to thoroughly evaluate various potential decisions, you can often arrive at the right decision with no outside assistance. When you're stressed or abruptly confronted with a decision, you're often not in the best frame of mind to make a responsible decision. It never hurts to slow down and take some time to reflect on a personal decision before taking premature action, which may come back to bite you.

You Make the Call

1. List five personal decisions you've made in the past six months.
2. List a personal decision you've made in the past six months that had a positive consequence or end result.

Religious Advisers

Certain types of personal and religious decisions require prolonged soul searching. For example, say you have a close friend who has started using drugs. He's trying very hard to get you to try them, but you're definitely not interested. You really enjoy his friendship, but you're afraid that if you mention his drug use to your parents, they'll make you terminate your friendship and tell your friend's parents all about their son's drug use. If you mention it to your school counselors, your friend will be expelled, and your friendship will be over. After much soul searching, you decide to talk to your family's religious adviser, who, fortunately, is also your friend's family's religious adviser. You explain your fear that your friend may end up moving on to even more dangerous drugs and emphasize that you really value your friendship. The adviser reassures you that your conversation will be kept in strict confidence. In a religious adviser you may find a welcoming, empathetic listener who may be willing to help you arrive at the best decision available. You must be very aware, however, that it is also possible that the best decision may involve legal consequences for your friend.

In the event that you don't know anyone associated with a given religion, you might consider asking your friends or relatives for a referral. Advisers who demonstrate a great deal of empathy are often very good choices when you're looking for guidance and direction.

These individuals, willing to assist you with your personal decisions, are driven by generosity and not selfish motives. You should ask them right away if the information you share will be kept completely private.

Consider this entirely different situation. Maybe you're really torn about what to do regarding the seventeen-year-old boy you've been secretly seeing, whose race differs from yours. You know your parents would be furious if they were to discover your relationship. You really like this boy, and you're desperate to find someone who can help you decide what to do. You finally decide to discuss your situation with your family's religious adviser. You explain how seriously you feel about this boy and that you're really afraid of what your parents' reaction will be if they find out about your relationship. You indicate that while you respect your parents a great deal, you are in total disagreement with their prejudices and opinions concerning interracial dating and marriage. Here you've made a tough decision to seek guidance from a religious adviser regarding what approach to consider in this very emotional issue. You hope that your religious adviser will be able to assist you in some way.

You Make the Call

1. List three hypothetical decisions where you feel a religious adviser might be of assistance.

Financial Decisions

You're eighteen and want to purchase your first car. You've found a perfect $2,800 used vehicle with low mileage and in good mechanical shape. You already have your driver's license and your parents' approval, with only one stipulation: you yourself must pay for all the costs of buying and maintaining your car. Now you have to determine what your costs will be and if you can afford them on your part-time income of $400 a month. This is a true financial decision that will require you to research car-ownership costs. A preliminary decision that you'll probably want to make is to have the car thoroughly evaluated by a competent mechanic to determine whether the vehicle is truly in as good shape as you've been led to believe. This evaluation, in writing, will be either a green light to go ahead with your cost analysis or a red light to stop your analysis right up front. You may not want to spend $150 to $300-plus dollars for an evaluation of a car that you think is in great shape. But this mechanic's report could end up saving you hundreds and maybe even thousands of dollars in future repair bills if the car has some hidden problems that you don't know about or can't see by simply test-driving the car. Buying this car will probably be your first large financial decision, and caution is always a good idea.

After you've determined that the car is very sound, you must undertake some research. You'll have to find out what your costs will be for the following: down payment, insurance, maintenance and upkeep, gasoline, parking and toll fees, and monthly car payment. You have the $800 down payment saved, but something your parents will have to do is secure a car loan in their name. You're worried that they may say no, but if you want the car, you'll have to approach them about the subject. If they agree, you'll have to commit to a timely monthly payment to cover the payments they'll have to make to the lending institution.

Whatever decision you ultimately arrive at, you'll know that you've done your very best to minimize the potential for unforeseen problems. In addition, you've taken a giant step toward becoming an adult in your parents' eyes, and you've given yourself the best opportunity for a successful outcome. This example should show you that buying your first car is a huge financial decision that also easily qualifies as a complex decision with many parts to it.

You Make the Call

1. List two situations in which you've made financial decisions in the past thirty days.
3. Explain how you arrived at the aforementioned decisions.
4. Discuss how the financial decisions you've made in the past month have affected your life.

Research Tools

Many decisions will require you to know specific information and research questions you can't answer. Two of the very finest resources for finding answers to specific questions are the Internet and your local library. The Internet, in particular, can provide a tremendous amount of specific information on just about anything. When you do research online, you should do your very best to validate the sources of the information you find. Realize that there are biased sources on the Internet that may give only one side of an argument or intentionally disseminate misinformation. You have to decide what is acceptable for your research purposes and what is only biased reporting. Checking out the sources or credentials is of critical importance. Never forget that your ultimate decision is only as good as the information you used to make the decision in the first place. Furthermore, it's you who will be held to account for any decision you make—not the Internet source.

The public library is also an exceptional resource, whether you have access to a computer or not. Some people prefer using information in hard-copy format instead of information on a computer screen. The information you find in a library may come from either a computer or from books. Be aware that libraries still have some books with information that is not contained in Internet files, even though the amount of information not available on the Internet is constantly dwindling.

You Make the Call

1. Name and talk about one decision you've made that required you to do some fact finding and/or research.
2. What research tools have you used to make a decision in the past two weeks?
3. How important do you feel proper research is when making difficult decisions?

Decision Counselors and Good Friends

Sometimes, prior to coming to a decision, you may want to discuss the subject with your school counselor or a good friend, both people you feel you can trust to keep your best interests at heart. For example, perhaps you're midway through your junior year and are really concerned about what decision you're going to make about going to college. Your parents have always insisted that you'll be going to college, no questions asked. You, however, don't necessarily share that view, and you need to discuss your decision process with someone other than your parents, who have only one goal in mind. You decide to discuss your options with your high-school counselor, who you feel will be more objective. Although you love and respect your parents, you feel that on this particular subject they have tunnel vision and are unable to consider that you may not want to take the college route. After your meeting with the counselor, you know you made the right decision to consult him about your future decisions. He has been very helpful in discussing some of the advantages of going to college as well as the advantages of going to a trade school or the military. He also suggested some ideas for a possible discussion with your parents, which you really found helpful.

Consider a different example. Maybe you're seriously considering getting a small tattoo on your left ankle, but you know your parents will probably never consent to it. You've become very close in the past six months with another senior girl, and you decide to ask her how she ever got her parents to allow her to get the small tattoo she has on her right shoulder. She totally surprises you by telling you that her parents didn't care if she got a tattoo. And then she shocks you by saying that she wishes her parents had cared and stopped her from getting it in the first place. Your close friend now wishes she had never gotten the tattoo. She says she has to change what she wears whenever she goes places where her tattoo might embarrass her. She points out that you should listen to your parents on this one and forget all about tattoos. She says it's the worst decision she's ever made, and she really regrets it. She can't wait until she can afford to have it removed, even though it will be a costly process. After hearing this from your friend, you still think tattoos are really cool, but you decide to wait until you get out of high school and see how you feel about the idea at that time.

A third-party opinion can be very refreshing at times and exactly what the doctor ordered. A friend can provide valuable feedback and insight that will help you reach the best decision possible. You may recall the old adage that two heads are better than one; many times, a second opinion will be all you need to make a sound decision.

You Make the Call

1. List two examples of decisions (other than those mentioned in this book) where you think a school counselor might make a difference in providing advice.
2. Discuss a decision you feel comfortable sharing where you consulted with a close friend before arriving at a final decision.

Artificial-Deadline Decisions

In order to accomplish certain goals or personal objectives, you may want to create an artificial deadline by which you must complete a project or come to a decision regarding a project. For example, maybe you've been postponing getting in shape for the past six months, so you commit yourself to an artificial starting deadline of January 10 to kick off your one-hour daily workouts. Here you're making a commitment to work out daily in the future based upon a decision you are making today. Artificial-deadline decisions, when made with conviction and commitment, can be tremendously helpful in accomplishing many of your goals and objectives. You just have to have the discipline and commitment to follow through.

Learn from Your Bad Decisions

You should be willing to look back at the consequences or fallout from your bad decisions in the past. Your first step should be to recognize when you've made a mistake and do your very best to figure out why your decision was bad. Was it a matter of not taking enough time to make the best decision possible? Was it a matter of not being willing to ask others for their feedback before you made your decision? Were you preoccupied with other things, such as your cell phone, allowing those distractions to limit your focus and preventing you from getting the decision correct the first time? Maybe you were too apathetic or lazy to bother trying to get it right the first time. Maybe you failed to place enough importance on your need to make a good decision, because you figured it really didn't make that big of a difference to the end result.

As you can see, there are many reasons why you might make a bad decision; those mentioned here are only a small sample. It is critical that you be willing to acknowledge your poor decisions and make a concerted effort to correct or improve your decision-making process whenever possible. You should try to make a habit of immediately acknowledging to yourself when you've made a poor decision and mentally evaluating what you could have done better or differently to get a better outcome. If you can, isolate what you did wrong and pinpoint how you can do a better job or make a better decision next time. Of course, this is easier said than done, but the first step in preventing yourself from making the same mistake a second time is to acknowledge it in the first place. Once you've learned why the decision was a mistake, you're in a good position to change your approach or thinking in order to arrive at a better decision in the future. Despite all this advice, you should realize that we all make bad decisions in our lifetimes. Often it is through our mistakes that we learn and grow. You should simply try to make fewer bad decisions as you grow into adulthood.

You'll be doing yourself a huge favor if you make a conscious effort to avoid making the same mistake a second time. This is a decision that will pay huge dividends in your future and brighten your entire life.

Examples of Bad Decisions

Bullying others—no exceptions	Drinking and driving
Speeding	Disrespecting others
Stealing someone's identity	Boating without a lifejacket on
Dropping out of high school	Stealing
Cheating	Lying and behaving deceitfully
Deciding not to do your homework	Sexting
Using illegal drugs	Sexually harassing others

Don't leave the scene of an accident when authorities need to ascertain responsibility and ask potential witnesses what happened. An obvious exception would be where authorities are unavailable and someone needs urgent medical care.

It's always a bad decision to participate in illegal activity when you know full well that your actions will possibly harm others, the environment, or you.

You Make the Call

1. Name three bad or poor decisions you've made in the past month.
2. List the consequences of your bad decisions.
3. Discuss what you learned from your bad decisions.
4. Name two poor decisions you've made in your lifetime that you regret and would do differently if you had to do them over again.
5. Discuss two good decisions you've made recently and explain what the consequences were.

Decision Diary

A superb idea is to use a spiral notebook as a diary in which you can record all your good and bad decisions, as well as the primary factors that were involved in the outcomes. The small amount of time you devote to writing down the details and outcomes of your decisions could result in a huge payoff now or later in your life. A decision diary is a detailed roadmap of where you've been and where you're going. When you're able to look back over the past few months and years and read about the decisions that have shaped your life, you'll be able to better understand what you did wrong and what you did right. Your decision diary could assist you in positively charting the course of your future decisions. And don't forget to record the consequences of your decisions, which are often the measuring stick of whether your decisions were good or bad. You probably need to record only your more important decisions and what your rationale was for making those decisions. You might also note what resources you chose to use and from whom, if anyone, you sought advice. Always keep in mind that your decisions and their outcomes will determine the future course of your life.

You Make the Call

1. Discuss how you think a decision diary could help you make better decisions in the future.

Judgment Decisions and Judgment Calls

When a problem has no clear-cut solution, you have to make a decision based on your best judgment. For instance, maybe your parents have agreed to let you make your own decision regarding your school lunches. You can either take your lunch, which your mother would prepare, or buy lunch in the school cafeteria. You really like the sandwiches and other goodies that your mother packs in your lunchbox, but most of your friends buy lunch at school, and the food is pretty good. You have to decide between these choices using your best judgment, keeping in mind that neither choice is right or wrong. The decision is yours—you make the call!

A judgment call is required when you have two seemingly equal solutions to a given problem and only one solution is required. For example, maybe your junior prom is only a month away, and you have to decide which of two girls to invite. You've dated both girls in the past year and enjoyed your time with both of them. You feel that both would be good choices for your date, but, in the end, you have to make a judgment call. Which one is it going to be? Making a final decision is not easy, but you have to choose one girl and hope you make the right decision. This judgment decision may require you to soul search and weigh subjective factors, which are either very hard or impossible to objectively evaluate. However, regardless of how difficult the choice may be, the final decision must be made by you. If you have the benefit of enough time to seek out the advice of others, you should by all means do so. Your past experiences and discussions with your friends and possibly your parents may be among your best resources to draw upon when making your final decision.

You Make the Call

1. Name one judgment call you've made in your lifetime.
2. Discuss the judgment call and what the consequences were.

Default Decisions

When you fail to come to a decision, by default you have allowed either circumstances or other individuals to make a decision for you. Let's assume that your sophomore homeroom class is having a car wash to raise money to help a student who has recently been in a horrible accident. The event is scheduled for Saturday at one o'clock in the supermarket parking lot, and the entire class is being encouraged to participate if they don't have other plans. You don't have other plans but figure you can simply not show up and let everyone assume you did have plans. By simply being absent at the car wash, you've made a default decision to not participate. As a consequence, fewer students have to carry the workload, and you may have a guilty conscience for not contributing to help someone in need.

In some cases, a default decision may result in the worst possible outcome, for which you might be held responsible since you failed to decide or act. For example, maybe your fourteen-year-old cousin is visiting from out of town, and you let her hang out with you and a couple of your sixteen-year-old friends. One of your friends is speeding, doing eighty-five in a fifty-five-mile-per-hour zone, and you choose to say or do nothing to slow your friend down and protect your young cousin and everybody else in the car. Your friend loses control of the car on a curve and ends up rolling it, resulting in severe injuries to your cousin, the driver, and one of your friends. Your default decision to say nothing will be held against you by your cousin, your aunt and uncle, and your parents for the rest of your life. And let's not forget the guilt you'll have to carry with you forever.

In other cases, you may intentionally allow a default decision if you've had a change of heart or if a situation changes beyond your control. For example, perhaps you were a member of the school band during your junior year. Over the summer, you lose your desire to be in the band your senior year. You're aware that the initial band meeting is scheduled for the first week of school, but you ignore it; by default, you've made a decision.

If you know that someone else will be held accountable if you make a default decision, you should take time to consider all the consequences, good and bad. Then you'll be able to make an informed default decision, as opposed to an irresponsible decision that shows no consideration for the situation or others' rights or responsibilities. The extra time and energy you spend looking at the rights of others before defaulting on a decision will pay huge dividends in the long run. Keep in mind that when all is said and done, a default decision ultimately results in a decision made by the circumstances, the situation, or someone else; don't make a habit of relying on default decisions, period. Don't allow yourself to become a bystander in decisions that affect your life—*you* make the decisions that affect your life!

You Make the Call

1. List a default decision you've made in the last year.
2. Discuss your reasons for making the default decision and what the consequences were for you and others.

Responsible-Party Decisions

You would be wise to always decide who is responsible for the decision in the first place. In some situations, you may not be the person responsible. For instance, maybe your trigonometry teacher puts you on a decoration committee charged with decorating the assembly hall for Christmas. You're one of twelve other students, including a student who is to act as the committee leader. Your work is going well when the school maintenance man, who is assisting with some of the more challenging decoration work, asks you if you want the decorations to be installed over some of the windows. You should immediately realize that this is not your decision and refer it to the head of the committee or your trigonometry teacher. In this situation, a simple question to ask yourself is who is responsible for the outcome of this decision. If your answer is anyone other than yourself, then the decision is not yours to make. You have a responsibility to point out whose decision it is and to either tell that person yourself or direct the person asking for a decision to the appropriate individual. If you delay, you may be held responsible for any resulting fallout.

You Make the Call

1. Name one responsible-party decision you're familiar with.
2. Explain why you feel it's important to tell the person responsible for making a decision about the situation as soon as possible.

Safety Decisions: Safety First, Always

Your own and others' safety should always be your primary concern when you consider any decision. You should work on developing an automatic response when confronted with any decisions involving safety. Ask yourself this question: Will making this decision harm others, their property, or me in any way, now or in the future? If your answer is a possible yes, you should take time to evaluate the risks and determine if this decision is worth making in the first place. In the event that your decision causes harm to others or you, you may well have to live with the outcome for the rest of your life. Furthermore, your accountability for your poor decision may include paying fines, losing important privileges, and losing personal freedom through incarceration. Whenever you're faced with a decision where safety is a concern, err on the side of caution and choose the safe alternative.

Get It Right the First Time

Get it right the first time: this is the cardinal rule when making any important decision. One of the best and harshest examples of not getting an important decision right the first time concerns the first-time meth user. When you decide to try meth, you sign your own death certificate. This is the type of decision you have to get right the first time; making the wrong decision can and will destroy your life and the lives of others.

Any type of decision that involves criminal activity should be placed in the category of "get it right the first time." When you hear a teenager talking from a jail cell about how he wishes he'd made a better decision about drugs, theft, assault, or murder, you're witnessing a real-life example of a young person who wishes from the bottom of his heart that he'd gotten it right the first time. In many of these cases, one bad decision ruined a life forever. When it comes to criminal activity, *always* get it right the first time! For the teenagers who don't get this message, the consequences could be life in prison or even death.

Consider a very different example. Maybe your teacher has given an assignment that requires you to prepare a paper on the assassination of President Kennedy. This paper must be at least 1,000 words in length and will make up 30 percent of your final grade. You are given six weeks to complete the assignment. You understand that this is your opportunity to make a big difference in your final grade, especially since you usually don't do well on tests. You decide to do it right by devoting yourself to writing a 1,500-word paper and truly going the extra mile. Your decision to do it right the first time pays off beautifully: you get the second-highest grade on the assignment. In this example, you decided that this was your opportunity to do something special that could make a real difference in your final grade. You could have chosen to do the minimum and receive an average grade, but you chose to give it your best, and your decision paid off handsomely. You realized that this decision had to be the correct one for you, because in this situation you would not be given a second chance to do better—it was now or never!

When you take the time to do things right the first time, your path to success in life becomes much easier, and your journey becomes far more fulfilling. In the long run, the extra time it takes to come to the best decision possible is returned in the form of time saved by not doing things a second or third time. When you make a habit of making the right decision the first time, you're putting forth your best effort each and every time you begin another project. Making the right decision the first time will yield many rewards, including fewer mistakes, higher achievement, and less regret. Of course, no one is perfect, and it's impossible to always get it right the first time. However, this is a goal that will take you a long way toward reaching your dreams.

You Make the Call

1. List two examples of decisions you've faced where getting it right the first time was very important.

2. Talk about the consequences of a decision you made where you did not get it right the first time.

3. Explain why you feel it's critical to always make the right decision the first time regarding criminal activity.

4. Discuss why you feel even one bad decision can change your entire future.

Do-Overs Are Rarely an Option

If you fail to make the right decision the first time, you'll find that do-overs are rarely an option. We've all had the horrible experience of making a poor decision and immediately wishing we could have a second chance. For example, maybe you have a Spanish midterm scheduled for Friday. Instead of studying the night before the big test, you decide to watch music videos with your boyfriend. The next day, the minute you finish the test, you wish you could go back to last night and change your decision. As we all know, we rarely get the chance to make a better decision, because do-overs are truly a very rare option. No matter how much you wish you could have a second chance, the fact remains that you'll have to live with the results of your decision, even if you'll regret it for a short while or for the rest of your life. It's often the most important decisions we wish we could do over again. But second chances are rare, and most decisions are final. Therefore, you must be realistic and acknowledge that the path your life takes may well be dictated by the end results of the decisions you make for yourself. Never, ever forget that only one bad decision, such as the decision to steal a car, can destroy your entire future!

Consider this example of a situation in which you are given the rare opportunity to make a better decision. Perhaps you chose to take a job right out of high school as a laborer with your city's parks department. After a year of doing mostly manual labor, you realize that your decision was a bad one and decide to enroll in your local community college to study computer programming. Here you had the opportunity to change the course of your future; the new decision replaces your original decision. Learn to ask yourself if the decision you're contemplating will be a final decision or if it will be the type of decision that will allow you to change or alter it later. But remember that most of the important decisions you make will be permanent. You should do your very best to get it right the first time, since you won't get a second shot.

You Make the Call

1. List two past decisions you've made that you wish you could revisit if you were granted a do-over.
2. Discuss what you've learned about do-over decisions in this guide.

Decision Recess

Whenever you find yourself facing a charged situation where your first inclination is to react emotionally, stop and take a decision recess. For example, maybe one of the guys at school took a revealing picture of you with his cell-phone camera when you were bending over to pick a book up from the floor. You didn't even know he'd taken the picture until later in study hall, when one of your friends tells you that it's on the Internet and that all the students are talking about it. You're absolutely furious and embarrassed on so many levels, and your first reaction/decision is to immediately hurt this guy in any way possible. Here, the best decision you can make is to remove yourself from the situation if at all possible by taking a decision recess. This is simply a cooling-off period for your mind and body during which you do your best to divert your thoughts to any other topic or idea. If at all possible, leave the area so that you can clear the cobwebs in your head. This cooling-off period may last from five minutes to a day or more; the time period is dictated by the gravity and emotion involved. It is imperative that you do your best to avoid making a decision when everything in your body screams for bloody revenge. A large percentage of the crimes committed in the United States are carried out when individuals allow their emotions to make decisions for them in moments of hatred, anger, and revenge. Once you've removed yourself physically and mentally from the situation, you can deal with it, however difficult it may be, in a better manner. Discuss your feelings with someone you trust if you feel his or her input would help. You want to strive toward a response as opposed to an emotional reaction. Do your best to respond and not react—your decision could change your life forever.

In a different example, maybe your bike has been stolen, and two months later you see the front wheel on the school bike rack, attached to a different frame. You are absolutely positive it's yours, because you see the small initials of your name where you scratched them when you got your bike last year. You're really mad and initially decide to wait until school gets out and confront whoever shows up to claim the bike. You want to physically confront the thief and do whatever it takes to get your front wheel back. You should take a decision recess after you have a friend look at the evidence and watch to see who comes to pick up the bike. This is a criminal matter, and you should let the police and your school's authorities handle it accordingly. Once again, as hard as it is to remove yourself from the situation, many times a decision recess is the best approach.

After you've had time to cool down, you can arrive at a decision. This means you'll be making a responsible, well-thought-out decision as opposed to a reactionary, shoot-from-the-hip, emotional decision.

You Make the Call

1. Discuss what you think a decision recess is and how it could help you in some of your future decisions.
2. Discuss the consequences of one decision you've made in the past where you should have taken a decision recess.

Final-Decision Checklist

Here's a list of questions you can use to evaluate most of your life decisions. Do yourself a huge favor and take the time to review this list whenever you're pondering any important decisions that may impact your future—you'll be glad you did!

1. Does this decision involve others' or my safety in any way?
2. Will I break or violate any law by making this decision?
3. How will this decision make me feel after I've made it?
4. Will I have remorse or regret after making this decision?
5. Am I the right person to make this decision in the first place?
6. Is this a decision for the short term or the long term?
7. Is this a decision that I should ask my parents about or have them seek professional or legal advice about before making?
8. Should I take a decision recess before making this decision?
9. Have I carefully considered all the possible consequences of making this decision at this time?
10. Am I rushing into a decision that I should be taking more time to research thoroughly?
11. Is this the same decision a prudent student would arrive at after reviewing all the facts?

12. Am I willing to accept full responsibility for any and all fallout from this decision?

13. Is this a domino decision that will necessitate future decisions, of which I am fully aware and willing and able to make?

14. Is this a decision that must be resolved at this time?

15. If appropriate, have I utilized the smart student's decision tool to arrive at this decision?

16. Have I done my homework and thoroughly researched this decision, if required? Am I satisfied that I've done my best to arrive at the very best decision possible?

17. Is this a life-changing decision that is so important to my future that I feel I absolutely must get it right?

Examples of Great Decisions

Choosing to go to college, trade school, or the military

Saving 10 percent or more of every paycheck you earn

Helping those less fortunate than you

Exercising regularly

Pursuing self-improvement in all areas

Investing your savings wisely

Expanding your horizons and constantly learning

Striving to enhance your mental, physical, and spiritual well-being

Eating healthy foods

Conclusion:
The Decisions Are Yours to Make

The information presented here on the types of decisions and the decision-making process will assist you in your life journey. Ideally, it will give you direction and focus when you face decisions that will determine the paths you take and the outcome of your life. Do not for a minute allow yourself to assume that this is just another guide that will have no bearing on your future. If you take away only one point from reading this guide, let it be that your decisions will have a huge impact on your future. You can view every decision as a step toward your future, whether that step is positive, negative, or just a neutral nongrowth decision.

Years from now, when you look back over your life, you'll want to see that your decisions moved you in the right direction toward a happy, successful, and productive life. You'll want to enjoy the outcomes of the positive decisions you've made over the years. No one is perfect, and not all of your decisions will have positive results, but your goal should be to make more positive than negative decisions. Yes, when all is said and done, we all have a scorecard that is imaginary on one hand and very real on the other. All your decisions will ultimately be added and subtracted, resulting in a sum total that will be a snapshot of your life. All your decisions have created the person you've become and determined what the future holds for you.

The decisions we make ultimately determine not only the people we'll become but also the lifestyles we'll live. Develop the habit of always thinking that your decisions are what create your present life as well as your future. The decisions you make today can and often will determine your entire future.

Decide Wisely

I hope you've taken the time to thoroughly read about the various types of decisions discussed in this guide. The information presented here can assist you in arriving at better and more positive decisions in your life. I highly recommend that you keep your copy of *Decisionology* available for handy reference whenever you face a decision for which the topics discussed here might be of service. Your future will be influenced in large part by your decisions. Decide wisely!

You Make the Call

1. What are two things you've learned from reading this guide?
2. Do your best to explain why the decisions you'll be making now and in the future can improve your chances for a happier and more fulfilling life.
3. Discuss one thing that reading this guide did for you personally.

Suggested Reading

The following books are highly recommended for anyone who wants to learn more about decision making and many other topics. I have found them to be extremely helpful in my quest for better understanding and enjoyment of life.

Helmstetter, Shad. *Choices.* New York: Pocket Books, 1989.

Helmstetter, Shad. *The Self-Talk Solution.* New York: Pocket Books, 1987.

Hopkins, Tom. *The Official Guide to Success.* New York: Champion Press, 1982.

Milteer, Lee. *Success Is an Inside Job.* Charlottesville, VA: Hampton Roads Publishing Company, 1996, 1998.

Mowen, John C. *Judgment Calls.* New York: Simon & Schuster, 1993.

Robbins, Anthony. *Awaken the Giant Within.* New York: Summit Books, 1991.

Rohn, Jim. *7 Strategies for Wealth & Happiness.* Rocklin, CA: Prima Publishing, 1985, 1996.

Russo, J. Edward and Paul J. H. Schoemaker, *Decision Traps.* New York: Simon & Schuster, 1989.

Waitely, Dennis. *Being the Best.* New York: Pocket Books, 1987.

About the Author

Daniel P. Gates is a native of Montana with a BS in business administration from the University of Montana and a teacher's certificate in business education. He has received numerous salesmanship awards, including salesman of the year, marketing director of the year, and million-dollar producer of the year, from various firms. He enjoys four-star movies, great music, horses, and fishing in Montana streams.

Index

reckless driving, *see* driving
regret, 16, 61, 79
relationships, 8, 36, 52, 68
    interracial, 55
    sexual, 22
    with friend's ex, 25–26
religious advisers, 54
research
    conducting, 5, 7, 45, 46
    tools, 58–59
resources, 38, 45, 46, 48, 58; *see also* guidance
responsibility; *see also* accountability
    for failure to act, 70
    for making decisions, 73
revenge, 35, 36, 81
rewards, 22–23
risks
    drunk driving, 2, 23
    evaluating, 31, 38, 71, 75
    in sexual relationships, 22
    taking, 15
    versus rewards, 22–23

S

safety concerns, 15, 27, 48, 50, 75
school; *see also* homework
    asking for tutoring help, 8–9
    choosing a college, 7, 60

dealing with bullies, 5–6
school band, 71
school counselors, 54, 60
second chances, 79–80
secret keeping, 8, 52
sexual relationships, 22
sexually transmitted diseases (STDs), 22
short-term decisions, 10–12, 39–40
simple decisions, 4–5
snap decisions, 42
soul searching, 40, 53, 54
speeding, 14, 16, 30, 70
spending decisions, 56–57
sports, 17, 39
stealing, 64, 79, 82
studying, *see* homework
swimming, 15–16

T

tattoos, 60–61
teachers, 3, 9
teeth brushing, 4
timing, 48
trade school, 7, 60
trust, 14, 23, 52, 60
tutors, 5

V

vocabulary, 20
volunteering, 36

W

wrong decisions, 2, 38, 63, 76